Best Sights to See at

Great Smoky Mountains National Park

By Rob Bignell

Atiswinic Press · Ojai, Calif.

BEST SIGHTS TO SEE AT GREAT SMOKY MOUNTAINS
NATIONAL PARK
A GUIDEBOOK IN THE
HITTIN' THE TRAIL: NATIONAL PARKS SERIES

Copyright Rob Bignell, 2017

Atiswinic Press
Ojai, Calif. 93023
dayhikingtrails.wordpress.com

ISBN 978-0-9961625-6-2

Cover design by Rob Bignell
Cover photo of view from Chimney Tops summit

Manufactured in the United States of America
First printing April 2017

For Kieran

Table of Contents

Introduction

I magine a place where several waterfalls tumble more than eight stories over ancient rock, where you can hike to a mountain vista offering 100-mile views, where countless streams and rivers rush over riffles and cascades through dense verdant forests, where you can traipse past historic pioneer buildings or stand in awe before a rare, majestic elk that haven't been seen in these parts since George Washington's time. The place is real: It's called Great Smoky Mountains National Park.

America's most visited national park, more than 10 million people annually enter the vast, sprawling mountainous terrain that crosses the states of Tennessee and North Carolina. The high visitation occurs in part because a sizeable number of Americans live within a day's drive. Great Smoky Mountains National Park's natural beauty and rich, preserved history, however, ensure it's a sparkling gem that's worth the road trip.

But with the park's incredible size of 816 square miles and the large crowds, how can you ensure that you see its main sights when vacationing or driving through? That's what "Best Sights to See at Great Smoky Mountains National Park" answers. This volume lists the top 10 most popular sights and details the top day hiking trails to best experience them.

Geology

One billion years ago, the area that now is the Great Smoky Mountains sat in an ocean at the edge of the North American continent. As clay, mud, sand and silt eroded off a nearby highlands, they filled the water, forming a layer nine-miles thick.

Much of the rock currently at the national park's surface are sedimentary layers that piled atop that layer over a span of 95 million years beginning about 545 million years ago. Fossils of sea creatures – burrows of worms and shells of crustaceans – can be found in these sedimentary layers at the park, most notably Cades Cove.

About 310 million years ago, the North American and African tectonic plates crashed into one another. For the next 65 million years, this grinding of plates pushed up land all along the North American coastline, creating the Appalachian Mountains, which stretched from New-foundland to Alabama. At one time, the Appalachians stood as high as the Rocky Mountains do today.

As the two tectonic plates separated and moved to their current positions, erosion began to tear down the Appalachians. Rivers and streams moved the sand and silt to the Atlantic Ocean and Gulf of Mexico; in fact, some of today's Gulf of Mexico beaches are made of eroded rock from what is now the Great Smoky Mountains.

The most resistant of those rocks – metasandstone – remain the park's highest peaks. The majority of waterfalls occur at metasandstone ledges.

In the millennia ahead, the Great Smoky Mountains eventually will erode away. Geologists estimate the park is losing about an inch of elevation every 500 years.

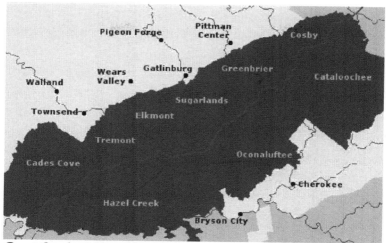

Great Smoky Mountains National Park straddles the Tennessee-North Carolina border.

Geography

The Great Smoky Mountains consists of several mountains with valleys tucked between them and the ridgelines leading to their peaks. For many Americans, it is synonymous with the Appalachians, though it is only a small part of it.

Among the oldest mountains in the world, the Appalachians stretch from Alabama northeast to Canada and so are much diverse geographically and culturally. The Southern Appalachians contain two ranges – Blue Ridge, which is to the northeast, and Unakas, which is to the Southwest. The widest part of the Unakas Range is the Great Smoky Mountains.

The Great Smoky Mountains also are almost the Appalachian's tallest, containing 16 peaks above 5000 feet. The higher elevations receive an average of 85 inches of precipitation annually.

That water drains off the peaks in more than 2100 miles of streams and rivers. All of it eventually reaches the Tennessee River, which flows into the Mississippi River.

The waterflow also has left an array of beautiful scenery – waterfalls, gurgling streams, deep valleys beneath high rocky peaks, gaps between the mountains where roads and trails run, and more.

Because of the elevation changes and the high precipitation, the Great Smoky Mountains holds five distinct ecosystems that support an incredible amount of biological diversity. More than 1500 flowering and 4000 non-flowering plants can be found there.

The vegetation exhales organic compounds that results in a blue mist often surrounding the park's peaks and hanging above its valleys. Appearing like smoke from a distance, the mountain range and park is named for this strikingly beautiful and perfectly safe mist.

History

The area has been long inhabited by Native Americans. One projectile found in the park dates to 9000 years ago.

When white settlers arrived in the late 1700s, Cherokees were the dominant tribe. They called Great Smoky Mountains *Shaconaqu* or "place of blue smoke."

As homesteaders settled the Great Smoky Mountains, the Cherokees viewed them as encroachers; after violence erupted, the Army intervention ensued. Following the Treaties of 1798 and 1819, Cherokees were forced to give up the mountains.

Then in 1838, the Army forcibly captured and moved Cherokees who refused to leave the Great Smokies. An estimated 4000 Cherokees died on the Trail of Tears in the relocation to Oklahoma. Still, some legally remained and became the Eastern Band of Cherokees.

White settlers of the Great Smoky Mountains mostly were of Scotch-Irish, English and German descent. Oconaluftee and Cades Cove were the first communities they established. Lumber companies followed in the late 1800s – some areas communities such as Smokemont, Tremont, Elkmont and Proctor initially were company towns – and they found great riches to be had. Some trees were so large that a single trunk filled a railcar.

Clearcutting left erosion and wildfires in its wake, however. As the primeval forest disappeared, a movement to preserve it arose. In 1923, businessman Willis Davis and wife Anne, who served in the Tennessee Legislature, proposed that the area be preserved as a national park. Congress authorized creation of the park three years later.

To actually have a national park, though, required the monumental task of purchasing 6000 separate tracts of land that would comprise the park. The effort quickly began in earnest during the 1920s.

By the 1930s on the sections of land purchased and preserved as a national park, the Civilian Conservation Corps constructed trails, fire towers, and other infrastructure. The Appalachian Trail later was built through the park on its way between Maine and Georgia.

One of the great ecological disasters in the park occurred during the first-half of the 20th century when blight, due to a fungus accidentally introduced from Asia, quickly wiped out whole groves of chestnuts. By the 1940s, the blight had destroyed about 4 billion trees nationwide.

The park received a boost in public interest during the 1950s when Disney filmed parts of its popular television series "Davy Crockett, King of the Wild Frontier" there.

During the early 2000s, park officials reintroduced a herd of elk to the park. Native elk had not graced the park since the late 1700s when overhunting and habitat loss doomed them in the Great Smoky Mountains.

Park Layout

Great Smoky Mountains National Park offers a number of access points and sections.

Most visitors enter through Gatlinburg, Tenn., which sits at the park's northcentral side. There's good reason to select Gatlinburg, as it leads to multiple scenic areas. Among them is the Roaring Fork Motor Trail, which offers trailheads to 80-foot Rainbow Falls and Mount Le Conte. The Sugarlands Visitor Center is west of that road and provides access to pretty Laurel Falls and the Elkmont and Tremont areas.

Gatlinburg also is the main way to reach another popular section of the park – Cades Cove. The cove is in the park's northwest. Nearby can be found a historic mill and farm site as well as the Cades Cove Nature Trail.

The Newfound Gap Road is the main north-south highway through the park, running from Gatlinburg to the Oconaluftee area. Along the way is Clingmans Dome (the highest point on the Appalachian Trail), Chimney Tops, the Alum Cave Trail, the Mingus Mill, and the Mountain Farm Museum.

From North Carolina, Bryson City serves as a major entry point to the park's southcentral section. Footpaths pass several streams with waterfalls, most notably the Deep Creek/Indian Creek Falls Trail.

Some less used access points include Fontana Dam in the park's southwest side, Hentooga Ridge Road, which runs past Balsam Mountain, Cataloochee, and Big Creek, all in North Carolina. Other Tennessee entries includes Cosby, Greenbrier (south of Pittman Center), and Townsend, which runs to either Cades Cove or Tremont.

How to Get There

Most begin the last leg of their journey to the Great Smoky Mountains from either Knoxville, Tenn., or Asheville, N.C. For either city, Interstate 40 heads to the park.

From Knoxville, take I-40 east/south. Exit south on Tenn. Hwy. 66, which merges with U.S. Hwy. 441. This runs through Gatlinburg to the park's northcentral entrance. Hwy. 441 cuts through the park over Newfound Gap.

From Asheville, go west/north on the interstate. Exit west/south on U.S. Hwy. 74 then head west/north on U.S. Hwy 19. In Cherokee, the road junctions with U.S. Hwy. 441, which can be taken north into the park and to Newfound Gap. To reach Bryson City, N.C., and its southcentral entry into the park, continue west on Hwy. 19.

Staying on I-40 from either city takes you to the park's eastern side. Several popular entrances to the park can be found along the way.

To reach the park's west side entrances, from Knoxville take U.S. Hwy 129 south. Exiting on N.C. Hwy. 28 heads to Fontana Dam.

When to Visit

The best months to day hike the national park are May through September. Depending on the year, April and October also can be pleasant.

As with the rest of the South, summers can be humid, especially July and August. Rain can occur during the afternoon even when the morning is sunny, so always check the weather forecast before heading out.

November through March usually is too cold for day hiking. Once snow falls, trails typically are used for cross-country skiing, snowmobiling or snowshoeing. Early spring often means muddy trails thanks to snowmelt and rainfall.

Kids Activities

A trip to Great Smoky Mountains National Park can be an educational experience for kids – though they may be having too much fun to even notice that they're learning!

The park delivers a variety of great activities that children can participate in from spring through autumn:

- **Ranger-led events** – Programs at several locations throughout the park focus on a range of interests, from wildlife and plants found in the Great Smoky Mountains to preserving local natural and cultural treasures. Among the most popular programs are the daily milling demonstrations at historic Mingus Mill and Cable Mill.

- **Junior Ranger Kids** – Kids between the ages of 5-12 can become a Junior Ranger. They'll first need to purchase a Junior Ranger booklet (available online, at any park

visitor center or at the Cades Cove or Elkmont campground) and complete its activities, and then they can receive a Junior Ranger badge. A Not-So-Junior Ranger program is available for teenagers.

• **Summer camps and workshops** – Family camps, nat-
uralist workshops, summer camps, hikes, and other ad-
ventures are available in the park at the Great Smoky
Mountains Institute at Tremont and the Smoky Mountain
Field School. Most require advanced registration.

Maps

To properly prepare for any hike, you should examine
maps before hitting the trail and bring them with you (See
the Bonus Section for more.). No guidebook can repro-
duce a map as well as the satellite pictures or topographical maps that you can find online for free. To that end, a
companion website to this book offers a variety of print-
able maps for each listed trail at *dayhikingtrails.wordpress.
com/trail-maps*.

The Cherokee entrance to Great Smoky Mountains National Park.

Best Sights

G reat Smoky Mountains National Park is so large that unless you spend years there, you won't see all it offers. So when you've only a week or so to visit the park, what are the absolute must-see sights? Following are the park's 10 best spots and the day hiking trails for getting to them.

Roaring Fork Motor Nature Trail leads to a number of delights, including the Rainbow Falls Trail.

Roaring Fork Motor Trail

Rainbow Falls Trail

For many Great Smoky Mountains National Park visitors, this narrow road – winding through a dense verdant forest past historic pioneer buildings – *is* the park. Easy to reach from Gatlinburg on the park's northcentral side, the one-lane loop offers a variety of outstanding sights, including log cabins, rushing creeks, and wildflowers. Without a doubt, though, the best sight is the national park's highest waterfall: Rainbow Falls.

The 5.4-miles round trip on the Rainbow Falls Trail does come with an asterisk – there are several other falls in the park that are taller, but Rainbow is the highest single-drop waterfall. To see it, you must traverse a 1500-foot gain in elevation, which is enough that temperatures will vary a few degrees between the parking lot and the falls.

To reach the trail, from U.S. Hwy. 441 in Gatlinburg, drive south on Historic Nature Trail, which becomes Cherokee Orchard Road as entering the park. These are parts of a set of roads that form the famous Roaring Fork Motor Nature Trail. After a couple of miles in the park, the road loops; once on that, look for Rainbow Falls parking lot signs.

The trail leaves from the lot's southwest corner at about 2575 feet elevation. It heads through an old-growth forest and in short order crosses the Trillium Gap Trail.

From there, the trail curves south over a boulder-strewn path and then parallels Le Conte Creek.

Portions of trail here are rocky, so be sure to wear a good pair of hiking boots and bring trekking poles.

The trail crosses the creek a few times, as well as two

tributaries. The gurgle of a number of cascades on the creek fill the air, and along the way you'll be sure to find some great spots to picnic.

Most of the cascades are due to the creek flowing down a steep grade. The trail actually is heading up a side of Mount Le Conte, the park's third highest peak. The ridge on the creek's north side is the mountain's Rocky Spur.

At last, the trail arrives at Rainbow Falls, which makes an 80-foot drop. The falls' lip sits at 4326 feet elevation, and a footbridge crosses the creek below the falls.

Spring marks the best time to see the falls, as the water flow will be the greatest. Mount Le Conte receives about eight feet of rain per year. It's also worth waiting for a sunny afternoon to make the trek, as a rainbow then forms in the mist, giving the trail its name.

Winter can offer its own delights, though, as ice formations sometimes build up around the falls during cold spells.

As tempting as it may be, stay off the rocks near the waterfalls. They are slick from the mist and algae, and over the years several people have fallen off them to their deaths.

Turn back at the waterfalls. If you have some extra energy, you can continue on to Mount Le Conte, however, for an additional 8-miles round trip and a significant ascent.

Bonus tip: If you bring a camera with you to catch a picture of the falls, leave early in the morning. The sun's position in the late morning and early afternoon will adversely effect the photo, and a number of other hikers are likely to get into your shot.

Rainbow Falls, at 80 feet, is the national park's highest single-drop waterfall.

Laurel Falls, which tumbles 80 feet over a few drops, is the park's most-visited waterfall.

Laurel Falls

Laurel Falls Trail

In large part because of the strenuous hike, most park visitors eschew Rainbow Falls for one that's much easier to reach and is quite impressive in its own right: picturesque 80-foot Laurel Falls. It's unquestionably the national park's most visited waterfall.

The Laurel Falls Trail runs 2.6-miles round trip and gains a mere 314 feet in elevation. During peak season, get to the trailhead early, as the parking lot for the popular trail quickly fills up. For great photos, hike early morning or late in the day, as the shade from the nearby mountains will prevent the water in your pictures from being washed out as reflecting sunlight.

To reach the trailhead, from Gatlinburg, take U.S. Hwy 441/Newfound Gap Road south. Turn left/west onto Fighting Creek Gap Road. Upon reaching Fighting Creek Gap, watch for a parking lot on right/north side. The trail leaves from the center of the lot's north side.

One of the reasons this trail remains popular is that the section leading to the impressive waterfalls is paved. Built during 1932 so fire crews could quickly reach the Cove Mountain area if needed, erosion quickly became a problem, and the trail was paved. Still, due to the steep grade and rough pavement, it's not suitable for strollers or wheelchairs.

The trail heads through a pine-oak woods with hemlock and beech along the stream, making for a colorful walk in autumn. May also is impressive, as mountain laurel blooms along the trail and near the falls, which runs its highest that month.

Within short order, the trail crosses Pine Knot Branch then begins to parallel Laurel Branch. Wooden posts appear every 0.1 miles so that you know far you've come.

Deer, often with fawns, wood squirrels, and songbirds are common on the trail. Be aware that black bears do live in the area and sometimes can be seen from the walkway; don't litter – including tossing apple cores – along the trail, as this attracts the bears.

The waterfall on Laurel Branch is magnificent, consisting of an upper and a lower section. A wide walkway crosses the stream where the mist from the falls roils over her head.

Stay off the rocks near the falls, as they are slippery due to mist and algae. In addition, the trail sports steep drop-offs, especially close to the falls, so keep an eye on children.

For those with a little extra energy, the trail continues past the waterfall to an old fire tower on Cove Mountain's summit. The tower is 4-miles round trip from the parking lot.

Other Great Smoky Waterfalls

Great Smoky Mountains National Park is a great destination for waterfall lovers. All across the park, the steep grade of rivers and creeks has carved down to erosion-resistant layers that suddenly drop-off. A few waterfalls top 90 feet in height.

Most of these can be reached via a day hike. They include:

• **Ramsey Cascades** – Water spills over 100 feet of cascades, a great reward for the strenuous 8-mile round trip hike. Park at the trailhead along Greenbrier Road.

• **Juney Whank Falls** – The 90-foot falls, split into two sections, is easy to reach via the 0.8-mile round trip Juney Whank Falls Trail. Park at the end of Deep Creek Road north of Bryson City.

• **Hen Wallow Falls** – The Gabes Mountain Trail runs 4.4 miles round trip to the 90-foot falls. Park in the lot designated for hikers at the Cosby Picnic Area.

• **Mouse Creek Falls** – The 45-foot falls can be reached via the 4-mile round trip Big Creek Trail near Cataloochee, N.C. Park at the Big Creek Trailhead on a gravel road off of Waterville Road.

• **Grotto Falls** – The 25-foot falls awaits at the end of the Trillium Gap Trail, a 3-mile round trip hike through old-growth hemlocks. Park at the trailhead off of the Roaring Fork Motor Nature Trail.

• **Abrams Falls** – Though a short drop of only 20 feet, the ferocity of the water tumbling over the falls is impressive. The trailhead for Abrams Falls Trail is just past Stop No. 10 on the Cades Cove Loop road.

• **Mingo Falls** – The area's best falls – at 120 feet the tallest in the southern Appalachians – actually sits just outside of the park on the Cherokee Indian Reservation in North Carolina. Take the Pigeon Creek Trail for 0.4-miles round trip from the Mingo Falls Campground to the falls.

Cades Cove

Cades Cove Nature Trail

Another of the most scenic drives in the park heads to Cades Cove, an isolated mountain valley that is a popular destination thanks to many well-preserved pioneer buildings. A campground, several historic structures, and the several trails heading into the surrounding mountains can be found there. Yet, while incredibly beautiful now, Cades Cove looked quite different to the pioneers who first settled it. That's because the chestnut – one of the trees that those settlers depended upon – has since largely disappeared.

Park visitors can hike through what once a grove of majestic chestnut trees on the Cades Cove Nature Trail, a 1.4-miles round trip trail, including the walk from the parking lot to the trailhead.

To reach the trail, from the park's Townsend Entrance Road in Tennessee, go right/west on Laurel Creek Road. The scenic highway heads straight into Cades Cove. Once there, go left/south into the Cades Cove Campground and park at the ranger station.

From the lot's southwest corner, walk south alongside Campground Drive. The road curves east. As it begins to curl north, look for the Cades Cove Nature Trail trailhead on the right/east.

A short stem trail leads to the main loop. Where the loop begins, continue straight/southeast. The loop is about a half-mile.

In the 1800s, the mountainsides of Cades Cove looked dramatically different than today. At that time, nearly a third of the forest surrounding Cades Cove consisted of towering chestnut trees. During spring, the chestnut blossoms made the mountainsides appear as if they were covered in snow. Each autumn, settlers could stand knee-deep in chestnuts. Many of the trees had diameters of nine to ten feet.

As the trail comes to Cooper Branch, which it crosses four times, there are no chestnuts to be seen. These days, oak, dogwood, sourwood and pine dominate.

What killed the chestnuts? Blight, from a fungus accidentally introduced from Asia, quickly wiped them out. By the 1940s, the blight had killed about 4 billion trees nationwide.

After the last crossing, the trail winds away from the creek to an overlook about 60 feet above the creek. Look along the way for spindly chestnut saplings, all that remain of the once mighty groves.

The loss of the chestnuts greatly changed life in the valley. Lumber from the tree, which was considered straight-grained and durable, no longer could be sold. Many settlers also had incorporated the sweet chestnut into their diets and gathered them for sale in nearby urban markets.

Animals suffered as well from the collapse of the chestnut groves. The fall nuts were a source of high calories for bears. They now rely on the less nutritious acorn for food.

From the overlook, the trail winds down the small hill then rejoins the stem. From there, retrace your steps back to the parking lot.

Despite the loss of the chestnut tree, the trail is still beautiful. Dogwoods bloom in spring while the sour-

A buck leaps a fence at historical Cades Cove.

woods and maples turn red in autumn.

Note that older maps and literature refer to this route as the Vista Trail.

Newfound Gap Road

Chimney Tops Trail

The major highway crossing the national park is New-found Gap Road, which is U.S. Hwy 441, running nearly 32 miles from south of Gatlinburg to Oconoluftee, N.C. Several waysides on the road allow you to hike short distances into the mountain valleys. Among the most impressive sights along the road, however, are the tops of those surrounding peaks.

On one of those sights, you can hike to a rare rock summit and be rewarded with some of the best views around via the Chimney Tops Trail.

The 2-mile one-way trail includes a steep 1700-foot gain in elevation. The good news is that in December 2014 the National Park Service completed a major refurbishing of the trail that included adding 367 rock steps – each weighing 300 pounds – and 291 locust log steps – most of them weighing about 80 pounds – which ensure a stable route.

To reach the trailhead, from Gatlinburg take the New-found Gap Road (aka U.S. Hwy. 441) south into the national park. Signs point to the Chimney Tops parking lot, which is more of a pullout; note that the trailhead's parking lot actually is a few miles south of the Chimney Tops campground.

The hike begins on the lot's northwest side, immediately entering the lush woodland at about 3490 feet elevation. In quick order, the dirt trail crosses the West Little Prong Pigeon River, whose boulders send the water churning and cascading. It then crosses the Road Prong, a

The Chimney Tops are among the remains of a collision 310 million years ago between North America and Africa.

small stream that flows into the aforementioned river.

For a while the trail loosely parallels the Road Prong before crossing it again to the stream's flatter and broader east side. After making one more crossing, at 0.9 miles, the Road Prong Trail intersects with the Chimney Tops Trail. Go right/north to stay on your trail.

From there, the trail ascends nonstop. In just half a mile, you'll reach 4400 feet elevation.

The home stretch sometimes feels like more of a rock climb than a hike as the trail breaks into the open over the stone. The rocks were folded upward about 310 million years ago when the North American and African plates collided, a geological event that resulted in the entire Appalachian Mountain range. Since then, natural weathering has eroded the top soil and exposed the hard slate, phyllite and metasiltstone.

The Chimney Tops consist of twin peaks. The trail reaches the higher of the pair first. At a little over 4724 feet elevation, the views are impressive to say the least.

To the north is the river valley where you parked your vehicle with Balsam Point towering beyond it at 5818 feet. The Sugarland Mountain massif (which the Chimney Tops are part of) rises in the west and south. To the southeast is Mt. Mingus at 5802 feet and then to the northeast is Peregrine Peak at 5375 feet. Directly north of Peregrine Peak and almost straight east from Balsam Point are the highest points in the region, the triple summits of Mount La Conte, the tallest of which is the easternmost at 6593 feet.

Chimney Tops' second peak, only about 20 feet lower than the first, also offers great views, but the real exhilaration is heading over the narrow rocks with the steep drops to either side to reach it.   > NO

Returning down the mountain to the parking lot can be tough. You may need to scoot down some of the rocks on your butt.

The hike can be difficult for younger children, who will find the steep climb taxing and likely will need to be carried at least part of the way. Teenagers, however, are capable of handling the hike and will find reaching the top a confidence-builder.

Clingmans Dome

Clingmans Dome Trail

The other fantastic mountain top along the Newfound Gap Road is Clingmans Dome, where you can enjoy views of up to a hundred miles atop one of the highest points east of the Mississippi River.

The 1-mile round trip Clingmans Dome Trail heads to the highest point in Great Smoky Mountains National Park and Tennessee and the third tallest east of the Mississippi. At 6625 feet, Clingmans Dome also is the highest point along the 2175-mile Appalachian Trail.

The road to Clingmans Done typically is open only from April through November. Autumn leaves usually change about mid-October, offering a spectacular red, orange and yellow display, but be aware that at this high elevation snow can fall as early as September.

To reach the trailhead, from the Newfound Gap Road, just 0.1 miles south of Newfound Gap, turn on to Clingmans Dome Road. Scenic pullouts with impressive views of ridges and valleys line the 7-mile highway. At the road's end is a large parking area for the trail, which begins at the visitor center.

The paved but steep 0.5-mile trail heads to a 54-foot observation tower at the summit. The elevated trail and the tower itself has a space-age feel with its curved paths and flying saucer-like observation platform.

Still, the top rewards with fantastic 360 degree views. On clear days, 100-mile views are possible. Tennessee is to the north and west while North Carolina is to the south and east. A verdant spruce-fir forest sits at the ridge tops while in autumn the multi-colored leaves of hardwood below adds swaths of harvest colors.

Unfortunately, a couple of obstructions can limit the views. The natural impediment is clouds. Due to the high elevation, precipitation at the summit is common.

The man-made barrier is air pollution. It can limit views to less than 20 miles. Due to air currents, pollution from vehicles, factories and other sources sometimes flow above the Great Smoky Mountains.

The view from Clingmans Dome is likely to change in the decades ahead. The invasive balsam woolly adelgid threatens stands of Fraser fir, which used to be the dominant tree at the park's highest elevations. Meanwhile, the hemlock woolly adelgid is wiping out hemlock trees across the park; the latter bug's devastating effects can be seen along Newfound Gap Road. In just a few decades, the existing forest will be replaced by younger trees of other species with a number of open areas where berry plants thrive.

Besides the disappearing view, another good reason to hike Clingmans Dome are the fantastic sunrises and sunsets. The latter time can be crowded, though, as those hoping to photograph the stunning scenery often line up for some 45 minutes before the sun sets.

Final notes: While the trail is paved, it is too steep for wheelchairs. In addition, pets and bicycles are not allowed on the trail.

Temperatures at Clingmans Dome usually are at least 10 F and sometimes 20 F cooler than the lowlands, so be sure to bring a sweatshirt or jacket.

Bonus trivia: The two highest points east of the Mississippi River are about 70 miles away, as the crown

The view from the top of Clingmans Dome can reach up to 100 miles on clear days.

flies, in North Carolina's Mt. Mitchell State Park. They are Mt. Mitchell (6,684 feet) and Mt. Craig (6,647).

Alum Cave

Alum Cave Trail

Between Chimney Tops and Clingmans Dome is another fantastic sight along Newfound Gap Road: a pair of cave-like formations with breathtaking vistas along the way.

The 4.4-miles round trip Alum Cave Trail sports an elevation gain of 1120 feet but is well-worth the effort. In fact, the trail is so popular during autumn and on any weekend with pleasant weather, that you'll want to arrive early or you won't find a parking space.

To reach the trailhead, from Gatlinburg, drive south on Newfound Gap Road/U.S. Hwy. 441 for about 10 miles; look for parking lot on left/east for the Alum Cave Trailhead. The dirt-packed trail starts at 3830 feet elevation in the Grassy Patch and immediately crosses Walker Camp Prong.

For the next mile, the trail heads through an old-growth forest of hemlock and yellow birch alongside Alum Cave Creek. The grade is gentle.

It then turns north and follows the Styx Branch, a tributary of Alum Cave Creek. During summer, rhododendron blooms here, making for an impressive sight.

At 1.3 miles, the trail reaches the first cave-like formation, Arch Rock. Freezing and thawing created the arch by eroding away the softer rock beneath the harder black slate. The trail goes under the arch, and steel cables sometimes serve as handrails. Hikers take stone steps out of Arch Rock.

From there, the trail crosses the Styx Branch and becomes fairly steep.

Alum Cave is a clay buff with a concave wall.

At 1.9 miles, the trail reaches Inspiration Point, an out-cropping at 4700 feet elevation. It offers great views. To the west is Little Duck Hawk Ridge; the Eye of the Needle, a hole in the rock at the ridge's top, can be seen from here as well. To the northeast is Mount Le Conte, the sixth highest peak east of the Mississippi River.

Peregrine falcons – locally called duck hawks – can be spotted flying about in the area. In fact, the trail's destination sits just below the aptly named Peregrine Peak.

At 2.2 miles, the trail arrives at Alum Cave. Not truly a cave but a bluff of orange clay with a concave wall that stretches 80 feet high and close to 500 feet long, it technically is known as a rock shelter.

Water often drips off the black slate ledges above, and during winter, icicles will form and drop, making this a dangerous stop during the colder months.

The cave takes its name from the alum that was mined there during the mid-1800s. A company dug out Epsom salt as early as 1838; this was used as a reddish brown dye for clothing. The Confederate Army in the 1860s mined saltpeter from the cave to manufacture gunpowder.

Sitting at 4950 feet elevation, the cave offers excellent views of the surrounding countryside. The trail can be taken all the way to the summit of Mount Le Conte (even better vistas are to be had on the climb up), but for a day hike the cave makes a good spot to turn back.

Other trail reports often claim the route can be muddy and with tree roots difficult to walk. While those reports are accurate, in 2015 the trail got a much needed makeover, repairing sections where erosion and landslides had caused damage.

Mountain Streams
Deep Creek/Indian Creek Falls Trails

More than 2900 miles of streams and rivers rush down the mountains and across valley floors at the national park. Because of the streams' steep grades, they often cut down to erosion-resistant rock, resulting in postcard-perfect ribbons of water over riffles. Many drop over ledges to form waterfalls.

Among the best ways to enjoy these scenic streams is a combination of the Deep Creek/Indian Creek Falls Trails. Two small waterfalls and a series of small cascades sit in the park's south-central section near Bryson City.

The Deep Creek/Indian Creek Falls trails are an easy walk over fairly flat terrain. The 1.6-mile round trip also is much less crowded than the national park's popular Laurel Falls area.

Spring marks the best time to hike the route; with snowmelt and rain, the waterfalls will be more spectacular, and you'll also miss all of the noise from innertubers heading downstream during the summer swelter. Autumn also is nice with fall leaf colors in September and October, but water flow will be diminished.

To reach the trailhead, from Bryson City take West Deep Creek Road (aka Route 1337) into the park via the Deep Creek Entrance. The parking lot sits where West Deep Creek and Tom Branch roads meet near the Deep Creek Campground. From the lot, walk back onto Deep Creek Road and go left/northeast into the turnaround; there, the Deep Creek Trail heads northwest into the woods.

The trail is an old road paralleling Deep Creek, so it's a

solid and wide walking surface. Hemlock, oak and pine trees line the route.

In short order, the trail comes to the Juney Whank Falls Trail intersection. Continue straight/northeast, where the trail comes alongside Deep Creek.

Wildflowers dot the ground beneath the tree canopy. During May and April, expect to see flame azalea in bloom; in May look for mountain laurel, and in June keep an eye out for rhododendron.

Hikers will soon hear the roar of the first waterfalls, where Tom Branch meets Deep Creek. A bench near the creek provides an opportunity to rest as enjoying the 60-foot-high Tom Branch Falls.

After the trail veers north, it crosses Deep Creek via a footbridge, offering views of cascades from both railings, then heads northeast again. Deep Creek now is on the trail's left.

Don't be surprised if you spot wildlife on the walk. Eastern cottontail rabbit, groundhogs, river otter, and white-tailed deer all inhabit the region. Also present but much more elusive, as they keep to themselves, are black bear, bobcat, coyote, red fox, red wolf, and wild boar.

As the creek and the trail curve northwest, you'll reach the Indian Creek Trail intersection. Go right/east onto it; Indian Creek flows on the trail's left side.

In no more than 200 feet, the trail reaches a spur leading to picturesque Indian Creek Falls. Take the short spur to the falls, which cascades about 25 feet down a series of ledges into a wide pool. Keep children off the rocks, which can be wet and slippery.

After taking in the falls, return the way you came.

Indian Creek Falls rambles 25 feet down several ledges.

Mingus Historic Grist Mill
Mingus Creek Trail

There is no shortage of historic sites to see in the national park. Among the most popular are clusters of them near the Sugarlands Visitor Center southeast of Gatlinburg and those in Cades Cove. One of the less visited but equally impressive sites is the Mingus Historic Grist Mill in the park's North Carolina section.

A 4-miles round trip, the Mingus Creek Trail segment runs past both the historic grist mill and a pioneer cemetery. The route is part of the Mountains-to-Sea Trail, a 1,000-mile footpath that runs from Clingmans Dome to the Outer Banks. It's also only a mile or so north of the Blue Ridge Parkway's southern/western entrance.

To reach the trailhead, from Cherokee, N.C., take U.S. Hwy. 441/Newfound Gap Road north to the Ocon-aluftee Visitor Center. Continue past the center for about half-a-mile to Mingus Mill, which is on the left/west. The trailhead is at the parking lot's far west end.

For the first mile, the wide, well-maintained trail follows an old road built by the CCC during the Great Depression. A canopy of new-growth forest covers the route, and rhododendron lines several sections of the trail. Early spring offers the chance to see a number of wildflowers on the forest floor; among them are blue phlox, violets, Virginia bluebells and white trillium.

About 0.1 miles from the trailhead, the historic grist mill is on the left/southeast. Built in 1886, it's still in operation today. Tours are available from mid-March through mid-November, and cornmeal ground on the site can be purchased. Though water-powered like other mills of its day, it uses a cast iron turbine, rather than a water wheel, to turn its grinder.

Continuing on the trail, from the grist is a millrace and then a moss-covered sluice, on which water is diverted from Mingus Creek to the mill.

The creek and trail traverse a narrow valley. Mt. Noble to the south tops out at 4066 feet and is the highest point on the horizon. Mt. Stand Watie to the north is 3961 feet. Thomas Ridge looms to the west.

At 0.4 miles in, the trail passes the park ranger shooting range. From there, the path gradually narrows, and its surface grows rockier. Two small footbridges allow hikers to cross the creek.

A trail junction appears at about a mile from the trailhead. Continue on the trail that runs right/north. It heads uphill to an old family cemetery along Mingus Creek.

In another mile, the pioneer cemetery with 29 gravesites marked by fieldstones appears on the right/east. This actually is one of four cemeteries near the Mingus Creek Trail; one of the others is a slave cemetery (which is immediately north of the parking lot).

The cemetery marks a good spot to turn back. If continuing on, the trail heads to the top of the surrounding ridges.

The trail, creek and mill are named for John Jacob Mingus, the first white to settle within what is now the national park. He arrived in the Oconaluftee Valley during the 1790s when a young adult.

Once done hiking, you can continue the exploration of pioneer times by driving a half-mile south of the trailhead to the Mountain Farm Museum. There you can explore a

The historic grist mill at Mingus Creek dates to 1886.

farmhouse, barn, applehouse, springhouse and smoke-house, all built in the 19th century.

Elk Herd
Big Fork Ridge Trail

Though elk were once a common sight in the southern Appalachian Mountains, over-hunting and habitat destruction doomed them. In fact, North Carolina has not had any native elk since the late 1700s – until reintroduction efforts began in the national park during the early 2000s. Visitors now can see a rare herd of elk on the Big Fork Ridge Trail.

The 3.6-miles round trip segment of this popular trail sits in the Cataloochee Valley of the park's North Carolina section. Early morning and dusk during autumn marks the best time to catch the elk and their antics.

To reach the trailhead, from Interstate 40, take Exit 20 onto U.S. Hwy. 276 south. Next, turn right/west onto Cove Creek Road/Hwy. 1395 (in the park, it becomes Old Cataloochee Turnpike). Then go left/west onto Cataloochee Entrance Road; follow that road to its end, where there's a parking lot for the Big Fork Ridge Trailhead. The parking lot faces large meadows where you usually can spot elk.

Adult male elk weigh about 600-700 pounds and stand up to 4 feet at the shoulder, easily making them the largest animals in the national park. Female elk average 500 pounds. Be sure to bring binoculars, as the meadow is off limits to people.

September often marks the best time to hike the trail, as the bull elk gather females and the newborns have lost their spots so are easier to see. You may even get to hear a male elk bugling. If you don't see any elk, they're probably hanging out in the nearby forest.

After taking in the view of the elk, carefully cross the road, following the trail roughly southeast. The trail immediately crosses the Rough Fork and begins its ascent. Though gradual at first, you'll gain about 750 feet over the next couple of miles.

The trail heads through a mixed hardwood forest of maples, pine and mountain laurel with rhododendron in the understory, making for a beautiful autumn walk of yellow and red leaves. Along the walk, you may notice a number of dead giant gray trees; these are hemlocks, some standing a hundred feet tall, robbed of life by the hemlock woolly adelgid blight.

About 0.8 miles in, the trail crosses a stream that flows into Rough Fork.

At 1.8 miles, you'll reach the summit of Big Fork Ridge at about 3600 feet elevation. There are no views unless hiking late in autumn when the leaves have fallen. The summit marks a good spot to turn back.

You can continue on, however, and many backpackers do as part of a large loop that includes connecting trails. The Big Ridge Trail itself goes down the highlands' southside through a forest of sassafras and mountain laurel. Along the way, there are good views of Caldwell Fork Valley's northern end then a crossing of Caldwell Fork. The trail ends at 3.2 miles when it junctions with the Caldwell Fork Trail.

The Big Fork Ridge Trail often is used by horse riders and following a rain can be muddy.

*A pair of wild bull elk feed along the edge of a field in the
Cataloochee Valley.*

Appalachian Trail

Appalachian Trail, Fontana Dam to Shuckstack Lookout Tower segment

The longest hiking-only footpath in the world – the Appalachian Trail – runs 2158 miles between Maine's Mount Katahdin and Georgia's Springer Mountain. In all, seventy miles of the trail crosses the national park. Most of it is deep in the park's interior.

One very accessible section of the trail in the park can be found where it crosses the highest dam east of the Rockies on the way to a lookout tower.

The Appalachian Trail's Fontana Dam to Shuckstack Lookout Tower segment runs 8.2-miles round trip. Parts of the segments are very steep and strenuous.

To reach the trail, from Bryson City, head south/east on U.S. Hwy. 19, which becomes U.S. Hwy. 74. Eventually, N.C. Hwy. 28 joins the highway from the south/east. When Hwy. 28 splits to head north/west, exit on it. Upon reaching Fontana Dam Road/Hwy. 1245, turn right/east onto it. Follow the road until it dead ends in a parking lot at the dam.

Go north from the lot to the dam, taking the walkway onto the dam. The Appalachian Trail heads over it, so this is not a spot for anyone afraid of heights.

At 480 feet high, the dam stretches 2,365 feet long. Impounding the Little Tennessee River, the dam holds back water for 30 miles to form Fontana Lake. Construct-ion of the dam began in 1942 with it opening in late 1944.

Up the ridge

Once on the dam's other side, the trail technically enters

The Appalachian Trail crosses the Fontana Dam, just south of the national park. ⌐ NC

the national park. It veers northwest alongside Lakeview Drive W.; the road/trail roughly parallels the Fontana Lake shoreline.

In 0.6 miles from the parking lot near the end of Lakeview Drive W., the Appalachian Trail splits off to the left/west. From there, you begin a steep climb; the split from the road is at 1879 feet elevation, and more than a 2000-foot ascent awaits you over the next 3.5 miles. Most of the elevation gain, though, comes in the first two-thirds of the hike.

The trail essentially runs atop an unnamed ridge sandwiched between two other elevated hillsides – the Shuckstack Ridge to the east and the taller Twentymile Ridge to the west and north.

Though definitely on a narrow dirt path in the wilderness, don't worry about getting lost. A simple white line blazed on the trees indicates the AT.

The Appalachian Trail enters the park from the north at Davenport Gap; Fontana Dam marks the southern entry point. The park's tower at Clingmans Dome is the trail's highest point between Maine and Georgia. You can stay overnight for free off the trail in the park, unless you're thru-hiking – which the park service defines as starting at least 50 miles outside of the park with plans to go at least 50 miles beyond it; in that case, you'll need a permit.

Shuckstack Lookout Tower

At 3.6 miles from the trailhead, you'll reach the steepest portion of trail. Fortunately, it's short.

The unnamed ridge at its top joins Twentymile Ridge. About four miles into the hike, once atop Twentymile, you'll reach a three-way junction; go right/east onto the spur trail.

In 0.1 miles, you'll reach Shuckstack Lookout Tower, which sits at 4020 feet, just above Sassafras Gap. Constructed in 1934, it's one of three park fire towers still in operation. You can take 78 steps up 60 feet to the top; while generally safe, the steel tower is in need of repair with some steps missing, and the tower's wood floor is partially rotted.

If you do head up to the top, you'll be rewarded with incredible 360 degrees of the surrounding park. To the west are the Unicoi Mountains. The Great Smoky Mountains rise in the north and east. The Blue Ridge Mountains and Fontana Lake are to the southeast. The ridge you walked on with the Snowbird and Nantahala mountains beyond are to the south.

After taking in the sights, retrace you steps back down the ridge and across the dam to your parking lot.

Bonus Tip: Another segment of the Appalachian Trail in the national park that definitely should be tried is at Clingmans Dome.

Bonus Section:
Day Hiking Primer

You'll get more out of a day hike if you plan ahead. It's not enough to just pull over to the side of the road and hit a trail that you've never been on and have no idea where it goes. In fact, doing so invites disaster.

Instead, you should preselect a trail (This book's trail descriptions can help you do that.). You'll also want to ensure that you have the proper clothing, equipment, navigational tools, first-aid kit, food and water. Knowing the rules of the trail and potential dangers along the way also are helpful. In this special section, we'll look at each of these topics to ensure you're fully prepared.

Selecting a Trail

For your first few hikes, stick to short, well-known trails where you're likely to encounter others. Once you get a feel for hiking, your abilities, and your interests, expand to longer and more remote trails.

Always check to see what the weather will be like on the trail you plan to hike. While an adult might be able to withstand wind and a sprinkle here or there, for any children with you it can be pure misery. Dry, pleasantly warm days with limited wind always are best when hiking with children.

Don't choose a trail that is any longer than the least fit person in your group can hike. Adults in good shape can go 8-12 miles a day; for children, it's much less. There's no magical number.

When planning the hike, try to find a trail with a mid-point payoff – that is something you and definitely any kids will find exciting about half-way through the hike. This will help keep up everyone's energy and enthusiasm during the journey.

If you have children in your hiking party, consider a couple of additional points when selecting a trail.

Until children enter their late teens, they need to stick to trails rather than going off-trail hiking, which is known as bushwhacking. Children too easily can get lost when off trail. They also can easily get scratched and cut up or stumble across poisonous plants and dangerous animals.

Generally, kids will prefer a circular route to one that requires hiking back the way you came. The return trip often feels anti-climactic, but you can overcome that by mentioning features that all of you might want to take a closer look at.

Once you select a trail, it's time to plan for your day hike. Doing so will save you a lot of grief – and potentially prevent an emergency – later on. You are, after all, entering the wilds, a place where help may not be readily available.

When planning your hike, follow these steps:

• Print a road map showing how to reach the parking lot near the trailhead. Outline the route with a transparent yellow highlighter and write out the directions.

- Print a satellite photo of the parking area and the trailhead. Mark the trailhead on the photo.
- Print a topo map of the trail. Outline the trail with the yellow highlighter. Note interesting features you want to see along the trail and the destination.
- If carrying GPS, program this information into your device.
- Make a timeline for your trip, listing: when you will leave home; when you will arrive at the trailhead; your turn back time; when you will return for home in your vehicle; and when you will arrive at your home.
- Estimate how much water and food you will need to bring based on the amount of time you plan to spend on the trail and in your vehicle. You'll need at least two pints of water per person for every hour on the trail.
- Fill out two copies of a hiker's safety form. Leave one in your vehicle.
- Share all of this information with a responsible person remaining in civilization, leaving a hiker's safety form with them. If they do not hear from you within an hour of when you plan to leave the trail in your vehicle, they should contact authorities to report you as possibly lost.

Clothing

Footwear

If your feet hurt, the hike is over, so getting the right footwear is worth the time. Making sure the footwear fits before hitting the trail also is worth the effort. With children, if you've gone a few weeks without hiking, that's plenty of time for feet to grow. Check out everyone's footwear a few days before heading out on the hike.

If it doesn't fit, replace it.

For flat, smooth, dry trails, sneakers and cross-trainers are fine; but if you really want to head onto less traveled roads or tackle areas that aren't typically dry, you'll need hiking boots. Once you start doing any rocky or steep trails – and remember that a trail you consider moderately steep needs to be only half that angle for a child to consider it extremely steep – you'll want hiking boots, which offer rugged tread perfect for handling rough trails.

Socks

Socks serve two purposes: to wick sweat away from skin and to provide cushioning. Cotton socks aren't very good for hiking, except in extremely dry environments, because they retain moisture that can lead to blisters. Wool socks or liner socks work best. You'll want to look for three-season socks, also known as trekking socks. While a little thicker than summer socks, their extra cushioning generally prevents blisters. Also, make sure kids don't put on holey socks; that's just inviting blisters.

Layering

On all but hot, dry days, you should wear multiple layers of clothing that provide various levels of protection against sweat, heat loss, wind and potentially rain. Layering works because the type of clothing you select for each stratum serves a different function, such as wicking moisture or shielding against wind. In addition, trapped air between each layer of clothing is warmed by your body heat. Layers also can be added or taken off as needed.

Generally, you need three layers. Closest to your skin is

the wicking layer, which pulls perspiration away from the body and into the next layer, where it evaporates. Exertion from walking means you will sweat and generate heat, even if the weather is cold. The second layer provides insulation, which helps keep you warm. The last layer is a water-resistant shell that protects you from rain, wind, snow and sleet.

As the seasons and weather change, so does the type of clothing you select for each layer. The first layer ought to be a loose-fitting T-shirt in summer, but in winter and on other cold days you might opt for a long-sleeved moisture-wicking synthetic material, like polypropylene. During winter, the next layer probably also should cover the neck, which often is exposed to the elements. A turtleneck works fine, but preferably not one made of cotton. The third layer in winter, depending on the temperature, could be a wool sweater, a half-zippered long sleeved fleece jacket, or a fleece vest.

You might even add a fourth layer of a hooded parka with pockets, made of material that can block wind and resist water. Gloves or mittens as well as a hat also are necessary on cold days.

Headgear

Half of all body heat is lost through the head, hence the hiker's adage, "If your hands are cold, wear a hat." In cool, wet weather, wearing a hat is at least good for avoiding hypothermia, a potentially deadly condition in which heat loss occurs faster than the body can generate it. Children are more susceptible to hypothermia than adults.

Especially during summer, a hat with a wide brim is

useful in keeping the sun out of your eyes. It's also nice should rain start falling.

For young children, get a hat with a chin strap. They like to play with their hats, which will fly off in a wind gust if not fastened some way.

Sunglasses

Sunglasses are an absolute must if walking through open areas exposed to the sun and in winter when you can suffer from snow blindness. Look for 100% UV-protective shades, which provide the best screen.

Equipment

A couple of principles should guide your purchases. First, the longer and more complex the hike, the more equipment you'll need. Secondly, your general goal is to go light. Since you're on a day hike, the amount of gear you'll need is a fraction of what backpackers shown in magazines and catalogues usually carry. Still, the inclination of most day hikers is to not carry enough equipment. For the lightness issue, most gear today is made with titanium and siliconized nylon, ensuring it is sturdy yet fairly light. While the following list of what you need may look long, it won't weigh much.

Backpacks

Sometimes called daypacks (for day hikes or for kids), backpacks are necessary to carry all of the essentials you need – snacks, first-aid kit, extra clothing.

For day hiking, you'll want to get yourself an internal frame, in which the frame giving the backpack its shape is inside the pack's fabric so it's not exposed to nature. Such frames usually are lightweight and comfortable. External frames have the frame outside the pack, so they are exposed to the elements. They are excellent for long hikes into the backcountry when you must carry heavy loads.

As kids get older, and especially after they've been hiking for a couple of years, they'll want a "real" backpack. Unfortunately, most backpacks for kids are overbuilt and too heavy. Even light ones that safely can hold up to 50 pounds are inane for most children.

When buying a daypack for your child, look for sternum straps, which help keep the strap on the shoulders. This is vital for prepubescent children, as they do not have the broad shoulders that come with adolescence, meaning packs likely will slip off and onto their arms, making them uncomfortable and difficult to carry. Don't buy a backpack that a child will "grow into." Backpacks that don't fit well simply will lead to sore shoulder and back muscles and could result in poor posture.

Also, consider purchasing a daypack with a hydration system for kids. This will help ensure they drink a lot of water. More on this later when we get to canteens.

Before hitting the trail, always check your children's backpacks to make sure that they have not overloaded them. Kids think they need more than they really do. They also tend to overestimate their own ability to carry stuff. Sibling rivalries often lead to children packing more than they should in their rucksacks, too. Don't let them overpack "to teach them a lesson," though, as it can damage bones and turn the hike into a bad experience.

A good rule of thumb is no more than 25 percent capacity. Most upper elementary school kids can carry only about 10 pounds for any short distance. Subtract the weight of the backpack, and that means only 4-5 pounds in the backpack. Overweight children will need to carry a little less than this or they'll quickly be out of breath.

Child carriers

If your child is an infant or toddler, you'll have to carry him. Until infants can hold their heads up, which usually doesn't happen until about four to six months of age, a front pack (like a Snugli or Baby Bjorn) is best. It keeps the infant close for warmth and balances out your back-pack. At the same time, though, you must watch for baby overheating in a front pack, so you'll need to remove the infant from your body at rest stops.

Once children reach about 20 pounds, they typically can hold their heads up and sit on their own. At that point, you'll want a baby carrier (sometimes called a child carrier or baby backpack), which can transfer the infant's weight to your hips when you walk. You'll not only be comfortable, but your child will love it, too.

Look for a baby carrier that is sturdy yet lightweight. Your child is going to get heavier as time passes, so about the only way you can counteract this is to reduce the weight of the items you use to carry things. The carrier also should have adjustment points, as you don't want your child to outgrow it too soon. A padded waist belt and padded shoulder straps are necessary for your comfort. The carrier should provide some kind of head and neck support if you're hauling an infant. It also should offer back support for children of all ages, and leg holes should be wide enough so there's no chafing. You want to be able to load your infant without help, so it should be stable enough to stand that way when you take it off the child can sit in it for a moment while you get turned around. Stay away from baby carriers with only shoulder straps as you need the waist belt to help shift the child's weight to your hips for more comfortable walking.

Fanny packs

Also known as a belt bag, a fanny pack is virtually a must for anyone with a baby carrier as you can't otherwise lug a backpack. If your significant other is with you, he or she can carry the backpack, of course. Still, the fanny pack also is a good alternative to a backpack in hot weather, as it will reduce back sweat. Your fanny pack need not be large. A mid-size pouch can carry at least 200 cubic inches of supplies, which is more than enough to accommodate all the materials you need.

Canteens

Canteens or plastic bottles filled with water are vital for any hike, no matter how short the trail. You'll need to have enough of them to carry about two pints of water per person for every hour of hiking.

Trekking poles

Also known as walking poles or walking sticks, trekking poles are necessary for maintaining stability on uneven or wet surfaces and to help reduce fatigue. The latter makes them useful on even surfaces. By transferring weight to the arms, a trekking pole can reduce stress on knees and the lower back, allowing you to maintain a better posture and to go farther.

If an adult with a baby or toddler on your back, you'll primarily want a trekking pole to help you maintain your balance, even if on a flat surface, and to help absorb some of the impact of your step.

Graphite tips provide the best traction. A basket just above the tip is a good idea so the stick doesn't sink into mud or sand. Angled cork handles are ergonomic and help absorb sweat from your hands so they don't blister. A strap on the handle to wrap around your hand is useful so the stick won't slip out. Telescopic poles are a good idea as you can adjust them as needed based on the terrain you're hiking and as kids grow to accommodate their height.

The pole also needs to be sturdy enough to handle rugged terrain, as you don't want a pole that bends when you press it to the ground. Spring-loaded shock absorbers help when heading down a steep incline but aren't necessary. Indeed, for a short walk across flat terrain, the right length stick is about all you need.

Carabiners

Carabiners are metal loops, vaguely shaped like a D, with a sprung or screwed gate. You'll find that hooking a couple of them to your backpack or fanny pack useful in many ways. For example, if you need to dig through a fanny pack, you can hook the strap of your trekking pole to it. Your hat, camera straps, first-aid kit, and a number of other objects also can connect to them. Hook carabiners to your fanny pack or backpack upon purchasing them so you don't forget them when packing. Small carabiners with sprung gates are inexpensive, but they do have a limited life span of a couple of dozen hikes.

Navigational Tools
Paper maps

Paper maps may sound passé in this age of GPS, but you'll find the variety and breadth of view they offer to be useful. During the planning process, a paper map (even if viewing it online), will be far superior to a GPS device. On the hike, you'll also want a backup to GPS. Or like many casual hikers, you may not own GPS at all, which makes paper maps indispensable.

Standard road maps (which includes printed guides and handmade trail maps) show highways and locations of cities and parks. Maps included in guidebooks, printed guides handed out at parks, and those that are hand-drawn tend to be designed like road maps, and often carry the same positives and negatives.

Topographical maps give contour lines and other important details for crossing a landscape. You'll find them invaluable on a hike into the wilds. The contour lines' shape and their spacing on a topo map show the form and steepness of a hill or bluff, unlike the standard road map and most brochures and hand-drawn trail maps. You'll also know if you're in a woods, which is marked in green, or in a clearing, which is marked in white. If you get lost, figuring out where you are and how to get to where you need to be will be much easier with such information.

Satellite photos offer a view from above that is rendered exactly as it would look from an airplane. Thanks to

Google and other online services, you can get fairly detailed pictures of the landscape. Such pictures are an excellent resource when researching a hiking trail. Unfortunately, those pictures don't label what a feature is or what it's called, as would a topo map. Unless there's a stream, determining if a feature is a valley bottom or a ridgeline also can be difficult. Like topo maps, satellite photos (most of which were taken by old Russian spy satellites), can be out of date a few years.

GPS

By using satellites, the global positioning system can find your spot on the Earth to within 10 feet. With a GPS device, you can preprogram the trailhead location and mark key turns and landmarks as well as the hike's end point. This mobile map is a powerful technological tool that almost certainly ensures you won't get lost – so long as you've correctly programmed the information. GPS also can calculate travel time and act as a compass, a barometer and altimeter, making such devices virtually obsolete on a hike.

In remote areas, however, reception is spotty at best for GPS, rendering your mobile map worthless. A GPS device also runs on batteries, and there's always a chance they will go dead. Or you may drop your device, breaking it in the process. Their screens are small, and sometimes you need a large paper map to get a good sense of the natural landmarks around you.

Compass

Like a paper map, a compass is indispensable even if

you use GPS. Should your GPS no longer function, the compass then can be used to tell you which direction you're heading. A protractor compass is best for hiking. Beneath the compass needle is a transparent base with lines to help your orient yourself. The compass often serves as a magnifying glass to help you make out map details. Most protractor compasses also come with a lanyard for easy carrying.

Food and Water
Water

As water is the heaviest item you'll probably carry, there is a temptation to not take as much as one should. Don't skimp on the amount of water you bring, though; after all, it's the one supply your body most needs. It's always better to end up having more water than you needed than returning to your vehicle dehydrated.

How much water should you take? Adults need at least a quart for every two hours hiking. Children need to drink about a quart every two hours of walking and more if the weather is hot or dry. To keep kids hydrated, have them drink at every rest stop.

Don't presume there will be water on the hiking trail. Most trails outside of urban areas lack such amenities. In addition, don't drink water from local streams, lakes, rivers or ponds. There's no way to tell if local water is safe or not. As soon as you have consumed half of your water supply, you should turn around for the vehicle.

Food

Among the many wonderful things about hiking is that

snacking between meals isn't frowned upon. Unless going on an all-day hike in which you'll picnic along the way, you want to keep everyone in your hiking party fed, especially as hunger can lead to lethargic and discontented children. It'll also keep toddlers from snacking on the local flora or dirt. Before hitting the trail, you'll want to repackage as much of the food as possible as products sold at grocery stores tend to come in bulky packages that take up space and add a little weight to your backpack. Place the food in re-sealable plastic bags.

Bring a variety of small snacks for rest stops. You don't want kids filling up on snacks, but you do need them to maintain their energy levels if they're walking or to ensure they don't turn fussy if riding in a child carrier. Go for complex carbohydrates and proteins for maintaining energy.

Good options include dried fruits, jerky, nuts, peanut butter, prepared energy bars, candy bars with a high protein content (nuts, peanut butter), crackers, raisins and trail mix (called "gorp"). A number of trail mix recipes are available online; you and your children may want to try them out at home to see which ones you collectively like most.

Salty treats rehydrate better than sweet treats do. Chocolate and other sweets are fine if they're not all that's exclusively served, but remember they also tend to lead to thirst and to make sticky messes. Whichever snacks you choose, don't experiment with food on the trail. Bring what you know kids will like.

Give the first snack within a half-hour of leaving the trailhead or you risk children becoming tired and whiny from low energy levels. If kids start asking for them every few steps even after having something to eat at the last rest stop, consider timing snacks to reaching a visible land-mark, such as, "We'll get out the trail mix when we reach that bend up ahead."

Milk for infants

If you have an infant or unweaned toddler with you, milk is as necessary as water. Children who only drink breastfed milk but don't have their mother on the hike require that you have breast-pumped milk in an insulated beverage container (such as a Thermos) that can keep it cool to avoid spoiling. Know how much the child drinks and at what frequency so you can bring enough. You'll also need to carry the child's bottle and feeding nipples. Bring enough extra water in your canteen so you can wash out the bottle after each feeding. A handkerchief can be used to dry bottles between feedings.

Don't forget the baby's pacifier. Make sure it has a string and hook attached so it connects to the baby's outfit and isn't lost.

What not to bring

Avoid soda and other caffeinated beverages, alcohol, and energy pills. The caffeine will dehydrate children as well as you. Alcohol has no place on the trail; you need your full faculties when making decisions and driving home.

Energy pills essentially are a stimulant and like alcohol can lead to bad calls. If you're tired, get some sleep and hit the trail another day.

First-aid Kit

After water, this is the most essential item you can carry.

A first-aid kit should include:

• Adhesive bandages of various types and sizes, especially butterfly bandages (for younger kids, make sure they're colorful kid bandages)

• Aloe vera

• Anesthetic (such as Benzocaine)

• Antacid (tablets)

• Antibacterial (aka antibiotic) ointment (such as Neosporin or Bacitracin)

• Anti-diarrheal tablets (for adults only, as giving this to a child is controversial)

• Anti-itch cream or calamine lotion

• Antiseptics (such as hydrogen peroxide, iodine or Betadine, Mercuroclear, rubbing alcohol)

• Baking soda

• Breakable (or instant) ice packs

• Cotton swabs

• Disposable syringe (w/o needle)

• Epipen (if children or adults have allergies)

• Fingernail clippers (your multi-purpose tool might have this, and if so you can dispense with it)

• Gauze bandage

• Gauze compress pads (2x2 individually wrapped pad)

• Hand sanitizer (use this in place of soap)

• Liquid antihistamine (not Benadryl tablets, however, as children should take liquid not pills; be aware that liquid antihistamines may cause drowsiness)

• Medical tape

- Moisturizer containing an anti-inflammatory
- Mole skin
- Pain reliever (aka aspirin; for children's pain relief, use liquid acetaminophen such Tylenol or liquid ibuprofen; never give aspirin to a child under 12)
  - Poison ivy cream (for treatment)
  - Poison ivy soap
  - Powdered sports drinks mix or electrolyte additives
  - Sling
  - Snakebite kit
  - Thermometer
  - Tweezers (your multi-purpose tool may have this)
  - Water purification tablets

If infants are with you, be sure to also carry teething ointment (such as Orajel) and diaper rash treatment.

Many of the items should be taken out of their store packaging to make placement in your fanny pack or backpack easier. In addition, small amounts of some items – such as baking soda and cotton swabs – can be placed inside re-sealable plastic bags, since you won't need the whole amount purchased.

Make sure the first-aid items are in a waterproof container. A re-sealable plastic zipper bag is perfectly fine. As the Great Smoky Mountains sports a humid climate, be sure to replace the adhesive bandages every couple of months, as they can deteriorate in the moistness. Also, check your first-aid kit every few trips and after any hike in which you've just used it, so that you can restock used components and to make sure medicines haven't expired.

If you have older elementary-age kids and teenagers who've been trained in first aid, giving them a kit to carry as well as yourself is a good idea. Should they find themselves lost or if you cannot get to them for a few moments, the kids might need to provide very basic first aid to one another.

Hiking with Children: Attitude Adjustment

To enjoy hiking with kids, you'll first have to adopt your child's perspective. Simply put, we must learn to hike on our kids' schedules – even though they may not know that's what we're doing.

Compared to adults, kids can't walk as far, they can't walk as fast, and they will grow bored more quickly. Every step we take requires three for them. In addition, early walkers, up to two years of age, prefer to wander than to "hike."

Preschool kids will start to walk the trail, but at a rate of only about a mile per hour. With stops, that can turn a three-mile hike into a four-hour journey. Kids also won't be able to hike as steep of trails as you or handle as inclement of weather as you might.

This all may sound limiting, especially to long-time backpackers used to racking up miles or bagging peaks on their hikes, but it's really not. While you may have to put off some backcountry and mountain climbing trips for a while, it also opens up to you a number of great short trails and nature hikes with spectacular sights that you may have otherwise skipped because they weren't challenging enough.

So sure, you'll have to make some compromises, but the payout is high. You're not personally on the hike to get a workout but to spend quality time with your children.

Family Dog

Dogs are part of the family, and if you have children, they'll want to share the hiking experience with their pets. In turn, dogs will have a blast on the trail, some larger dogs can be used as Sherpas, and others will defend against threatening animals.

But there is a downside to dogs. Many will chase animals and so run the risk of getting lost or injured. Also, a doggy bag will have to be carried for dog poo – yeah, it's natural, but also inconsiderate to leave for other hikers to smell and for their kids to step in. In addition, most dogs almost always will lose a battle against a threatening animal, so there's a price to be paid for your safety.

Many places where you'll hike solve the dilemma for you as dogs aren't allowed on their trails. At Great Smoky Mountains National Park, dogs are verboten on all trails but two – the Gatlinburg and the Oconaluftee River trails.

If you can bring a dog, make sure it is well behaved and friendly to others. You don't need your dog biting another hiker while unnecessarily defending its family.

Rules of the Trail

Ah, the woods or a wide open meadow, peaceful and quiet, not a single soul around for miles. Now you and your children can do whatever you want.

Not so fast.

Act like wild animals on a hike, and you'll destroy the very aspects of the wilds that make them so attractive. You're also likely to end up back in civilization, specifically an emergency room. And there are other people around. Just as you would wish them to treat you courteously, so you and your children should do the same for them. Let's cover how to act civilized out in the wilds.

Minimize damage to your surroundings

When on the trail, follow the maxim of "Leave no trace." Obviously, you shouldn't toss litter on the ground, start rockslides, or pollute water supplies. How much is damage and how much is good-natured exploring is a gray area, of course. Most serious backpackers will say you should never pick up objects, break branches, throw rocks, pick flowers, and so on – the idea is not to disturb the environment at all.

Good luck getting a four-year-old to think like that. The good news is a four-year-old won't be able to throw around many rocks or break many branches.

Still, children from their first hike into the wilderness should be taught to respect nature and to not destroy their environment. While you might overlook a pres-chooler hurling rocks into a puddle, they can be taught to sniff rather than pick flowers. As they grow older, you can teach them the value of leaving the rock alone. Re-gardless of age, don't allow children to write on boulders or carve into trees.

Many hikers split over picking berries. To strictly abide by the "minimize damage" principle, you wouldn't pick any berries at all. Kids, however, are likely to find great pleasure in eating blackberries, currants and thimbleber-ries as ambling down the trail. Personally, I don't see any problem enjoying a few berries if the long-term payoff is a respect and love for nature. To minimize damage, teach them to only pick berries they can reach from the trail so they don't trample plants or deplete food supplies for animals. They also should only pick what they'll eat.

Collecting is another issue. In national and most state and county parks, taking rocks, flower blossoms and even pine cones is illegal. Picking flowers moves many species, especially if they are rare and native, one step closer to extinction. Archeological ruins are extremely fragile, and even touching them can damage a site.

But on many trails, especially gem trails, collecting is part of the adventure. Use common sense – if the point of the trail is to find materials to collect, such as a gem trail, take judiciously, meaning don't overcollect. Otherwise, leave it there.

Sometimes the trail crosses private land. If so, walking around fields, not through them, always is best or you could damage a farmer's crops.

Pack out what you pack in

Set the example as a parent: Don't litter yourself; whenever stopping, pick up whatever you've dropped; and always require kids to pick up after themselves when they litter. In the spirit of "Leave no trace," try to leave the trail cleaner than you found it, so if you come across litter that's safe to pick up, do so and bring it back to a trash bin in civilization. Given this, you may want to bring a plastic bag to carry out garbage.

Picking up litter doesn't just mean gum and candy wrappers but also some organic materials that take a long time to decompose and aren't likely to be part of the natural environment you're hiking. In particular, these include peanut shells, orange peelings, and eggshells.

Burying litter, by the way, isn't viable. Either animals or erosion soon will dig it up, leaving it scattered around the trail and woods.

Stay on the trail

Hiking off trail means potentially damaging fragile growth. Following this rule not only ensures you minimize damage but is also a matter of safety. Off trail is where kids most likely will encounter dangerous animals and poisonous plants. Not being able to see where they're stepping also increases the likelihood of falling and injuring themselves. Leaving the trail raises the chances of getting lost. Staying on the trail also means staying out of caves, mines or abandoned structures you may encounter. They are usually dangerous places. Finally, never take a shortcut on a switch-back trail. Besides putting them on steep ground upon which they could slip, their impatient act will cause the switchback to erode.

Trail Dangers

On Great Smoky Mountains trails, three common dangers face hikers – ticks, bears and poison ivy. Fortunately, these threats are easily avoidable.

Ticks

One of the greatest dangers comes from the smallest of creatures: ticks. Both the wood and the deer tick can infect people with Lyme disease.

Ticks usually leap onto people from the top of a grass blade as you brush against it, so walking in the middle of the trail away from high plants is a good idea. Wearing a hat, a long sleeve shirt tucked into pants, and pants tucked into shoes or socks, also will keep ticks off you, though this is not foolproof as they sometimes can hook onto clothing. A tightly woven cloth provides the best protection, however. Children can pick up a tick that has hitchhiked onto the family dog, so outfit Rover and Queenie with a tick-repelling collar.

After hiking into an area where ticks live, you'll want to examine your children's bodies (as well as your own) for them. Check warm, moist areas of the skin, such as under the arms, the groin and head hair. Wearing light-colored clothing helps make the tiny tick easier to spot.

To get rid of a tick that has bitten you or another in your hiking party, drip either disinfectant or rubbing alcohol on the bug, so it will loosen its grip. Grip the tick close to its head, slowly pulling it away from the skin. This hopefully will prevent it from releasing saliva that spreads disease. Rather than kill the tick, keep it in a plastic bag so that medical professionals can analyze it should disease symptoms appear. Next, wash the bite area with soap and water then apply antiseptic.

In the days after leaving the woods, also check for signs of disease from ticks. Look for bulls-eye rings, a sign of a Lyme disease. Other symptoms include a large red rash, joint pain, and flu-like symptoms.

If any of these symptoms appear, seek medical attention immediately. Fortunately, antibiotics exist to cure most tick-related diseases.

Bears

Bears live throughout the Great Smoky Mountains. Avoidance always is a better solution than being forced into a situation where you have to scare off an attacking bear. You can avoid them by staying out of bear areas in spring when they're awaking from hibernation or tending cubs. Typically bears will avoid us, but a mother who thinks her cubs are threatened more than likely will chase if not attack you. If you stumble across a bear with cubs, keep your distance and move away from them. Sometimes the mother will send her cubs up a tree as she watches to see if you are a threat; don't pass between her and that tree, or she'll attack.

Also, avoid berry patches in fall. If you notice signs of bears, like paw prints, droppings, demolished berry bushes, claw marks on trees, or the smell of carrion, you shouldn't continue onward.

If you do encounter a lone bear, don't turn your back to it but gather everyone in the group together in a single cluster, make as much noise as possible, and move slowly in opposite direction. Bears usually won't attack a group of more than four people.

Should you accidentally come face to face with a bear, you can try to scare it off. Jingling bells work well. You also can throw rocks at ground in front of the bear if it approaches, but this probably necessitates that you bend down, making you an easier target for a fast-moving animal. Pepper spray also will ward off a bear and can be conveniently holstered so it's easy to reach and use.

If attacked, don't run but play dead by lying on the ground, bringing your legs to your chest, tucking in your head, and covering the back of your neck with your hands. The bear might swat and sniff at you, but when it sees you're playing dead, it won't consider you a threat.

Poison ivy

Often the greatest danger in the wilds isn't our own clumsiness or foolhardiness but various plants we encounter. The good news is that we mostly have to force the encounter with flora. Touching the leaves of poison ivy in particular results in an itchy, painful rash. Each plant's sticky resin, which causes the reaction, clings to clothing and hair, so you may not have "touched" a leaf, but once your hand runs against the resin on shirt or jeans, you'll probably get the rash.

To avoid touching these plants, you'll need to be able to identify each one. Remember the "Leaves of three, let it be" rule for poison ivy. Besides groups of three leaflets, poison ivy has shiny green leaves that are red in spring and fall.

By staying on the trail and walking down its middle rather than the edges, you are unlikely to come into contact with this pair of irritating plants. That probably is the best preventative. Poison ivy barrier creams also can be helpful, but they only temporarily block the resin. This lulls you into a false sense of safety, and so you may not bother to watch for poison ivy.

To treat poison ivy, wash the part of the body that has touched the plant with poison ivy soap and cold water. This will erode the oily resin, so it'll be easier to rinse off. If you don't have any of this special soap, plain soap sometimes will work if used within a half-hour of touching the plant. Apply a poison ivy cream and get medical attention immediately. Wearing gloves, remove any clothing (including shoes) that has touched the plants, washing them and the worn gloves right away.

For more about these topics and many others, pick up this author's "Hikes with Tykes: A Practical Guide to Day Hiking with Kids." You also can find tips online at the author's "Day Hiking Trails" blog (*hikeswithtykes.blogspot. com*). Have fun on the trail!

Index

About the Author

Rob Bignell is a long-time hiker, book editor, and author of the popular "Hikes with Tykes," "Headin' to the Cabin," "Hittin' the Trail" and "Best Sights to See" guidebooks and several other titles. He and his son Kieran have been hiking together for the past decade. Rob served as an infantryman in the Army National Guard and taught middle school students in New Mexico and Wisconsin. His newspaper work has won several national and state journalism awards, from editorial writing to sports reporting. In 2001, The Prescott Journal, which he served as managing editor of, was named Wisconsin's Weekly Newspaper of the Year. Rob and Kieran live in Wisconsin.

CHECK OUT THESE OTHER HIKING BOOKS BY ROB BIGNELL

"Headin' to the Cabin" series:
◆Day Hiking Trails of Northeast Minnesota
◆Day Hiking Trails of Northwest Wisconsin

"Hikes with Tykes" series:
◆Hikes with Tykes: A Practical Guide to Day Hiking with Children
◆Hikes with Tykes: Games and Activities

"Hittin' the Trail" series:
Minnesota
◆Gooseberry State Park
Minnesota/Wisconsin
◆Interstate State Park (ebook only)
◆St. Croix National Scenic Riverway
Wisconsin
◆Barron County
◆Bayfield County
◆Burnett County (ebook only)
◆Chippewa Valley (Eau Claire, Chippewa, Dunn, Pepin counties)
◆Crex Meadows Wildlife Area (ebook only)
◆Douglas County
◆Polk County
◆Sawyer County
National parks
◆Best Sights to See at America's National Parks
◆Grand Canyon (ebook only)

ORDER THEM ONLINE AT:
dayhikingtrails.wordpress.com

Made in the USA
Lexington, KY
17 September 2017